WILLIAMS-SONOMA
E S S E N T I A L S
VINEGARS

WILLIAMS-SONOMA
E S S E N T I A L S

VINEGARS

GENERAL EDITOR
CHUCK WILLIAMS

RECIPES
ANN CREBER

PHOTOGRAPHY
PHILIP SALAVERRY

WILLIAMS-SONOMA
Founder: Chuck Williams

WELDON OWEN INC.
President: John Owen
Publisher: Wendely Harvey
Managing Editor: Jill Fox
Consulting Editor: Norman Kolpas
Design & Illustration: Brenda Duke
Editorial & Design Assistant:
  Marguerite Ozburn
Recipe Assistants: Cathie Graham,
  Janet Lodge
Proofreader: Meredith Phillips
Indexer: ALTA Indexing Service
Production: Stephanie Sherman,
  James Obata
Photography Assistant:
  David Williams
Food Stylist: Bruce Yim
Food Stylist Assistants:
  Barbara Bragle, Tim Scott
Prop Stylist: Amy Glenn

Production by:
Mandarin Offset, Hong Kong
Printed in China

A Weldon Owen Production

WILLIAMS-SONOMA ESSENTIALS
Conceived and produced by:
Weldon Owen Inc.
814 Montgomery Street
San Francisco, CA 94133
Phone number: (415) 291-0100
Fax number: (415) 291-8841
In collaboration with:
Williams-Sonoma
100 North Point Street
San Francisco, CA 94133

Copyright © 1994 Weldon Owen Inc.
All rights reserved, including the right
of reproduction in whole or in part in
any form.

Library of Congress
Cataloging-in-Publication Data:
Creber, Ann.
  Vinegars / recipes. Ann Creber ;
photography, Philip Salaverry.
    p.   cm. -- (Williams-Sonoma
essentials)
  Includes Index.
  ISBN: 1-875137-20-3
  1. Cookery (Vinegar) 2. Vinegar.
I. Series.
TX819.V5C74 1994
641.6'2--dc20   94-4154
                              CIP

ACKNOWLEDGMENTS
The publishers would like to thank
the following people and organiza-
tions for their assistance in lending
props for photography: The Attic;
Paul Bauer, Inc.; The Cannery
Wine Cellars; Cyclamen Studios,
Julie Sanders, Designer; Ward
Finer; Luna Garcia; Bea and Marty
Glenn; Nancy Glenn; Rosie Glenn-
Finer; Judy Goldsmith and Bernie
Carrasco, J. Goldsmith Antiques;
Missy Hamilton-Backgrounds;
Mimi Koch-Backgrounds;
L'Osteria del Forno; and Smith
and Hawken, Ltd.

WEIGHTS AND MEASURES
All recipes include customary U.S.
and metric measurements. The metric
conversions are based on a standard
developed for these books and have
been rounded off. The actual weights
may vary. Unless otherwise stated,
the recipes were designed for
medium-sized fruits and vegetables.

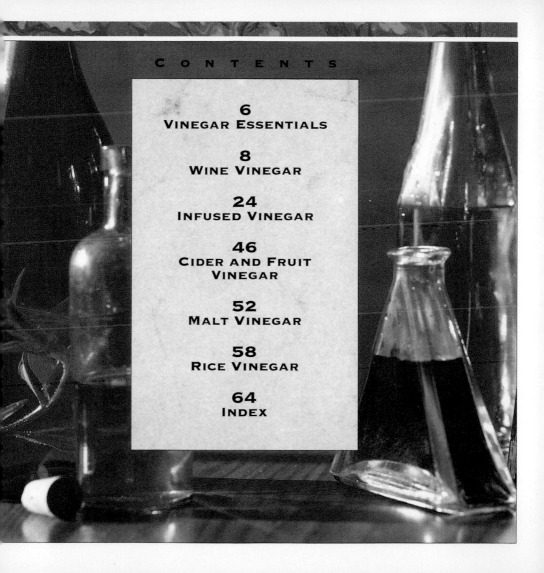

CONTENTS

6
VINEGAR ESSENTIALS

8
WINE VINEGAR

24
INFUSED VINEGAR

46
CIDER AND FRUIT
VINEGAR

52
MALT VINEGAR

58
RICE VINEGAR

64
INDEX

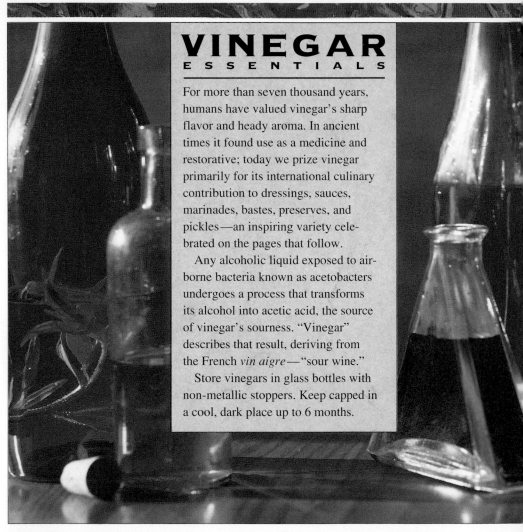

VINEGAR
ESSENTIALS

For more than seven thousand years, humans have valued vinegar's sharp flavor and heady aroma. In ancient times it found use as a medicine and restorative; today we prize vinegar primarily for its international culinary contribution to dressings, sauces, marinades, bastes, preserves, and pickles—an inspiring variety celebrated on the pages that follow.

Any alcoholic liquid exposed to airborne bacteria known as acetobacters undergoes a process that transforms its alcohol into acetic acid, the source of vinegar's sourness. "Vinegar" describes that result, deriving from the French *vin aigre*—"sour wine."

Store vinegars in glass bottles with non-metallic stoppers. Keep capped in a cool, dark place up to 6 months.

WINE VINEGAR

Vinegars made from wine rate among the most versatile in the pantry. Wine vinegars range from red and white wine versions, to sherry, Champagne, and balsamic varieties.

The best wine vinegars are slowly aged in oak barrels at a constant temperature of about 70°F (21°C). This method was perfected in the Middle Ages by early vinegar professionals in Orléans, France. If vinegar is slowly aged, the label will indicate "made by the Orléans Process."

Modern processes include dripping wine through casks and submerged fermentation. These methods produce less delicate—and less expensive— vinegars. Use delicate vinegars with fresh dishes, when their flavors will shine. For cooked dishes, the less delicate vinegars are perfectly acceptable.

RED WINE VINEGAR
Fine red wine vinegar is made from fine red wine. It is pale pink with the distinct aroma of the original wine. This vinegar complements robust salads and red meat dishes.

WHITE WINE VINEGAR
Good quality white wine vinegar is clear to pale gold in color and possesses a lightness best suited to simple dressings for vegetables, seafood and poultry. It makes a perfect base for the Infused Vinegars beginning on page 24.

CHAMPAGNE VINEGAR
Usually produced from a still white wine of France's Champagne region, good quality Champagne vinegar has a delicacy that complements seafood and poultry.

SHERRY VINEGAR
Produced from the fortified wine of Jerez, Spain, sherry vinegars have a full, mellow, slightly sweet flavor. The best are aged as long as 30 years. It is especially good in recipes containing sugar and honey.

BALSAMIC VINEGAR
True balsamic vinegar, labeled *aceto balsamico traditizionale,* is a speciality of Modena, Italy. Made from the reduced juice of sweet white grapes, it ages for a decade or longer in a progression of aromatic wooden casks. Purple-brown, sweet-sour and almost syrupy, balsamic vinegar has a beguiling complexity that makes it an almost magical culinary elixir. Use it sparingly in dressings and sauces.

BRUSCHETTA WITH ROASTED BELL PEPPERS

While any crusty bread can be used to make bruschetta, it's the durum wheat used in true Italian bread that gives this version its authenticity.

- 2   each *red and yellow bell peppers (capsicums), halved, stemmed and seeded*
- 3   *garlic cloves*
- 1   *1 lb (500 g) loaf coarse country-style Italian bread*
- 2   *tablespoons extra-virgin olive oil*
- 2   *tablespoons balsamic vinegar*
- 1   *cup (4 oz / 125 g) thinly shaved Parmesan cheese*

To roast peppers, preheat an oven to 400°F (200°C). Place peppers onto an ungreased baking sheet, flattening with hand. Place the garlic onto the same sheet. Roast 40 minutes, turning the peppers and garlic several times during cooking. Remove the peppers and garlic from the oven; reduce oven temperature to 350°F (180°C). Place the peppers into a paper bag, seal and set aside 20 minutes. Cut the bread into ½-inch (1.25-cm) thick slices. Cut large slices in half. Place onto an ungreased baking sheet and bake until lightly browned, 7–10 minutes. Peel and dice the peppers. Peel and mash the garlic. In a small bowl, combine the peppers, garlic, olive oil and balsamic vinegar. Mix until well blended. To serve, spread the pepper mixture onto the browned bread. Top with the cheese.

Makes 20 portions

ITALIAN BREAD SALAD

This traditional salad makes an excellent use of day-old crusty bread.

- 8 *thick slices coarse country-style Italian bread*
- 6 *large ripe tomatoes, sliced*
- 1 *cucumber, peeled and sliced*
- 1 *red (Spanish) onion, sliced*
- ¼ *cup (⅜ oz/10 g) chopped fresh basil leaves*
- 6 *tablespoons (3 fl oz/90 ml) virgin olive oil*
- 3 *tablespoons balsamic vinegar*
  Salt and freshly ground pepper

Soak the bread in cold water for a few minutes, then squeeze in hands to remove as much water as possible. Tear the bread into pieces and put it in a serving bowl. Add the tomatoes, cucumber, onion and basil. In a separate bowl combine the olive oil and balsamic vinegar and mix into the salad. Salt and pepper to taste. Chill in the refrigerator at least 1 hour. To serve, spoon onto individual plates.

Serves 4

Marbled Beet Soup

The light cream called for here has 18% butterfat. If that is not available, substitute equal parts half-and-half and whipping cream.

3   beets, peeled and cubed
4   cups (32 fl oz / 1 l) water
1   cucumber, peeled, seeded
*   and sliced*
2   cups (16 fl oz / 500 ml) rich
*   beef stock*
3   tablespoons balsamic vinegar
2   tablespoons lemon juice
*   Salt and freshly ground pepper*
1¼ cups (10 fl oz / 300 ml) light
*   (single) cream*
*   Fresh herbs, chopped*

Cook the beets in the water until tender, about 1 hour. Add the cucumber and cook 5 minutes. Pour into the work bowl of a food processor or blender. Add the stock, balsamic vinegar, and lemon juice. Salt and pepper to taste. Purée until smooth. Chill several hours. To serve, pour into a tureen. Gradually pour in the cream, swirling it for a marbled effect. Garnish with the herbs.

Serves 8–10

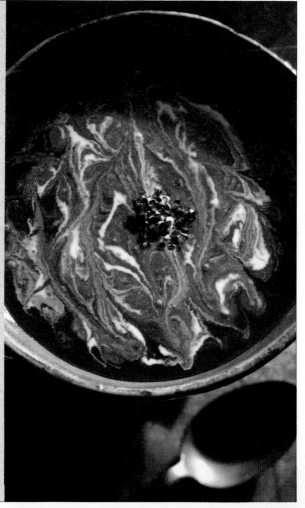

Gazpacho Sorbet

Sherry vinegar adds tang to this icy version of the classic Spanish soup.

1   *large tomato, peeled, seeded and chopped very finely*
2   *cups (16 fl oz / 500 ml) tomato juice*
1   *cucumber, peeled, seeded and diced*
1   *tablespoon shredded fresh basil*
1   *tablespoon finely chopped fresh parsley*
1   *teaspoon sugar*
⅓   *teaspoon freshly ground pepper*
3½ *tablespoons sherry vinegar*
1   *egg white, stiffly beaten*
3   *avocados, halved and pitted*

In a large bowl whisk together the tomato, tomato juice, cucumber, basil, parsley, sugar, pepper and 1½ tablespoons of the sherry vinegar. Fold in the egg white. Freeze until firm. To serve, brush the avocados with the remaining sherry vinegar and place onto individual plates. Scoop the frozen sorbet into the hollow of each avocado.

Serves 6

OYSTERS IN CHAMPAGNE VINEGAR SAUCE

Always keep fresh oysters on ice until serving time.

5   *dozen fresh oysters*
6   *shallots or 1 red (Spanish) onion, finely chopped*
½   *cup (4 fl oz/125 ml) Champagne vinegar*
1   *teaspoon coarse cracked pepper*
2   *tablespoons extra-light olive oil*
1   *tablespoon chopped fresh dill*
3   *tablespoons finely shredded white Japanese radish (daikon)*
3   *lemons, quartered*
    Fresh dill sprigs

Shuck the oysters and return to the half-shell. In a bowl combine the shallots or onions, Champagne vinegar, pepper, olive oil, dill and radish. Cover and chill until serving time. To serve, place the oysters in their half-shells on a serving platter. Spoon the sauce over each oyster. Garnish with the lemon quarters and dill sprigs.

Serves 6–8

Poached Chicken in Champagne Mayonnaise

The creaminess of this Champagne Mayonnaise enriches the delicate flavor of the chicken. Serve with carrot and jicama slices.

- 3 cups (24 fl oz / 750 ml) chicken stock
- 1 onion, sliced
- 1 celery stalk with leaves, sliced
- 1 carrot, sliced
- 12 peppercorns
- 7 sprigs fresh thyme
  Salt
- 6 chicken breast halves, skinned and boned
- 2 cups mixed greens

In a large pot combine the stock, onion, celery, carrot, peppercorns, 1 sprig of the thyme and salt to taste. Bring to a simmer. Add the chicken, cover and barely simmer until just opaque throughout, 25–30 minutes. Set aside. When cold, remove chicken. To serve, line individual plates with the greens. Slice each breast and arrange on top. Spoon the Champagne Mayonnaise along slices. Garnish with the remaining thyme sprigs.

Champagne Mayonnaise

- 2 egg yolks
- ½ teaspoon mustard powder
- ⅓ teaspoon salt
- ¼ teaspoon white pepper
- 3½ tablespoons Champagne vinegar
- 1 cup (8 fl oz / 250 ml) virgin olive oil
- 1 tablespoon boiling water

In a small bowl blend the egg yolks, mustard, salt and pepper. Using an electric mixer beat vigorously until light and fluffy. While continuing to beat, alternately add the Champagne vinegar and olive oil, pouring each in a thin trickle. When all of the oil is incorporated and the mayonnaise has thickened, beat in the boiling water. Chill until serving time.

Serves 6

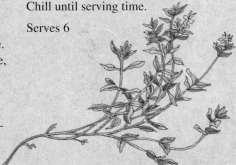

16

ROAST DUCKLING WITH KUMQUATS

This beautifully sharp-tasting sauce complements the richness of roast ducklings without overwhelming them. If kumquats are difficult to obtain, substitute mandarin orange segments.

- 2   2 lb (1 kg) ducklings
- 2   tablespoons vegetable oil
- ½   teaspoon salt
- 1   onion, peeled and quartered
- 1   carrot, peeled and halved
- 1   celery stalk, cut into 2-inch (5-cm) lengths
- 5   cups (40 fl oz / 1.25 l) chicken stock
- 20   kumquats
- ⅔   cup (5 oz / 155 g) sugar
- ⅔   cup (5 fl oz / 160 ml) red wine vinegar
- 6   tablespoons (3 fl oz / 90 ml) Grand Marnier
- 2   tablespoons each cornstarch and water

Preheat an oven to 375°F (190°C). Rub the ducklings all over with the oil and salt and place into a roasting pan. Surround with the onion, carrot and celery. Roast, basting occasionally, until tender, about 1½ hours. Remove the ducklings and vegetables from the pan and keep warm. Skim the fat from the pan juices. Add the stock and simmer 10 minutes. Strain and keep warm. Thinly slice 14 of the kumquats. Thickly slice the remaining kumquats and reserve. In a heavy saucepan combine the thinly sliced kumquats, sugar and red wine vinegar. Cook over medium heat until slightly carmelized. Whisk in the Grand Marnier and strained stock. Return to heat. In a separate bowl mix the cornstarch and water until blended. Slowly add to sauce, whisking constantly, until sauce comes to a boil. Reduce heat and simmer 5 minutes. Remove from heat and add one half of the reserved kumquats. To serve, cut the ducklings into portions, top with the sauce and remaining kumquat slices.

Serves 6

PEPPER-WRAPPED ITALIAN SAUSAGES

Based on a hearty peasant-style Italian recipe, this is a sturdy, well-flavored dish that is perfect for entertaining.

- 8 *spicy fresh Italian sausages*
  Juice of 1 fresh lemon
- ½ *teaspoon crushed red pepper flakes*
- 1½ *tablespoons white wine vinegar*
- ½ *teaspoon dried oregano*
- ⅓ *teaspoon freshly ground pepper*
- 4 *red bell peppers (capsicums), halved, stemmed, seeded, roasted and peeled (method on page 10)*
- 1 *green (spring) onion, chopped*

Preheat an oven to 375°F (190°C). Place the sausages into a shallow baking dish. Sprinkle with half of the lemon juice and the pepper flakes. Bake the sausages, turning occasionally, until browned and crisp-skinned, about 45 minutes. Drain well and keep warm. In a bowl mix together the remaining lemon juice, white wine vinegar, oregano and pepper. To serve, wrap each sausage in half a red pepper and place onto a serving platter. Pour the lemon juice mixture over the sausages. Garnish with the onion.

Serves 8

Chicken Roulades

If smoked chicken is not available, substitute sliced smoked turkey breast.

1 lb (500 g) smoked chicken
Lettuce leaves

Slice the chicken and arrange slices on top of the lettuce leaves on a serving platter. Spread the Pickled Grapes around the meat.

Pickled Grapes

2 lb (1 kg) seedless grapes, divided into small bunches
3 cups (1½ lb / 750 g) sugar
2 cups (16 fl oz / 500 ml) white wine vinegar
4 cloves
1 cinnamon stick
1 star anise

Put well-washed grapes into sterilized wide-mouthed jars. In a saucepan combine the sugar, white wine vinegar, cloves, cinnamon and star anise. Bring to a boil, boil 5 minutes, then pour the liquid over the grapes. Seal immediately. Store at least 2 weeks before using.

Serves 4

PORK WITH FIG SAUCE

8 dried figs, stemmed and chopped
¼ cup (2 fl oz / 60 ml) port wine
¼ cup (2 fl oz / 60 ml) water
6 tablespoons (3 oz / 90 g) unsalted
   butter
2½ lb (1.25 kg) pork tenderloin,
   trimmed of fat and halved
2 tablespoons red wine vinegar
2 tablespoons finely minced shallots
1½ cups (12 fl oz / 375 ml) light
   (single) cream

Soak the figs in the port 1 hour. Add
the water and 1 tablespoon of the butter. Simmer until softened, 20 minutes.
Transfer to the work bowl of a food
processor or blender and purée. In a
frying pan heat the remaining butter
and brown the pork, 5 minutes per side.
Reduce heat, cover and cook until just
pink, about 15 minutes. Remove meat
and keep warm. Deglaze the pan with
the red wine vinegar. Add the shallots
and cream and cook until thickened,
3 minutes. Remove from heat, stir in
the fig mixture and reheat. To serve,
slice and arrange the pork on the sauce.

Serves 6

I N F U S E D
VINEGAR

Steeping aromatic ingredients in vinegar imbues it with extra flavor and color to complement a wide variety of dressings, sauces and cooked dishes.

Use one of two basic methods to flavor vinegar. The most subtle-tasting results come from slowly infusing flavors in a sealed bottle or flavoring in minutes by simmering. For the quick method, use a saucepan that will not react with the vinegar's acidity.

Choose a base vinegar with less than 5% acidity to best showcase the taste of infused fruit and herbs. White wine vinegar works well.

Once the flavors have developed, transfer the vinegar to attractive glass bottles with nonmetal stoppers. Store vinegar 6 months on the pantry shelf. Be sure to make plenty to give as gifts.

BASIL VINEGAR

2   cups (16 fl oz / 500 ml)
    white wine vinegar
8   peppercorns
¾   cup (1 oz / 30 g) fresh
    basil leaves

In a sterile glass container combine the vinegar, peppercorns and basil, reserving a few leaves for bottles. Seal and set in a sunny spot, at least 10 days. Strain liquid and pour into sterilized bottles. Add the reserved basil leaves and seal. Makes 2 cups (16 fl oz/500 ml).

ORANGE VINEGAR

2 cups (16 fl oz / 500 ml)
   white wine vinegar
1 *1-inch (2.5-cm)*
   cinnamon stick
2 *cloves*
   Peel of 1 fresh orange,
   sliced

In a sterile glass container combine the vinegar, cinnamon, cloves and orange peel, reserving a few pieces of peel for bottles. Seal and set in a sunny spot, at least 1 week. Strain liquid and pour into sterile bottles. Add the reserved orange peel and seal. Makes 2 cups (16 fl oz/500 ml).

STRAWBERRY VINEGAR

2 cups (16 fl oz / 500 ml)
   white wine vinegar
¾ *cup (3 oz / 94 g) ripe*
   strawberries, stemmed
   and crushed
2 *teaspoons sugar*

In a sterile glass container combine the vinegar, berries and sugar. Mix lightly. Seal and set in a sunny spot to allow flavors to develop, at least 1 week. Strain the vinegar. If necessary, strain twice to ensure clarity. Pour into sterile bottles and seal. Note: Do not add strawberries to the bottles as they will disintegrate and make the vinegar cloudy. Makes 2 cups (16 fl oz/500 ml).

RASPBERRY VINEGAR

2 cups (16 fl oz / 500 ml)
   white wine vinegar
½ *cup (2 oz / 65 g) ripe*
   raspberries, rinsed
   thoroughly, dried and
   lightly crushed

In a sterile glass container combine the vinegar and raspberries. Seal and set in a sunny spot, 10 days to 2 weeks. Strain the vinegar. If necessary, strain twice to ensure clarity. Pour into sterile bottles and seal. Note: Do not add raspberries to the bottles as they will disintegrate and make the vinegar cloudy. Makes 2 cups (16 fl oz/500 ml).

GARLIC VINEGAR

2   cups (16 fl oz / 500 ml)
    white wine vinegar
8   peppercorns
5   garlic cloves, peeled
    and sliced

In a non-corrosive
saucepan combine the
vinegar, peppercorns and
garlic. Bring to a gentle
simmer and cook until
flavor has developed,
about 15 minutes. Cool.
Strain the liquid and pour
into sterile bottles and
seal. Makes 2 cups
(16 fl oz/500 ml).

PORCINI VINEGAR

2   cups (16 fl oz / 500 ml)
    white wine vinegar
1   small white onion,
    peeled and sliced
1   fresh thyme sprig
½   cup (1½ oz / 45 g) dried
    porcini slices

In a non-corrosive
saucepan combine the
vinegar, onion, thyme
and porcini, reserving
a few slices for bottles.
Bring to a gentle simmer
and cook until flavor
has developed, about
15 minutes. Cool. Strain
the liquid and pour into
sterile bottles. Add the
reserved porcini slices
and seal. Makes 2 cups
(16 fl oz/500 ml).

CHILI VINEGAR

2   cups (16 fl oz / 500 ml)
    white wine vinegar
1   garlic clove, peeled
    and sliced
10 small hot dried chilies

In a sterile glass container
combine the vinegar, gar-
lic and chilies, reserving
a few chilies for bottles.
Seal and set in a sunny
spot, up to 2 weeks. Strain
the liquid and pour into
sterilized bottles. Add
the reserved chilies and
seal. Note: Wash hands
immediately after han-
dling hot chilies. Makes
2 cups (16 fl oz/500 ml).

TARRAGON VINEGAR

2   cups (16 fl oz / 500 ml)
    white wine vinegar
½   cup (½ oz / 15 g) fresh
    tarragon leaves
12 peppercorns

In a non-corrosive saucepan, combine the vinegar, tarragon and peppercorns, reserving a few tarragon leaves and peppercorns for bottles. Bring to a gentle simmer and cook until flavor has developed, about 15 minutes. Cool. Strain the liquid and pour into sterile bottles. Add the reserved tarragon and peppercorns and seal. Makes 2 cups (16 fl oz/500 ml).

MIXED HERB VINEGAR

1½ cups (12 fl oz / 375 ml)
    white wine vinegar
½   cup (4 fl oz / 125 ml)
    red wine vinegar
8   peppercorns
½   cup (¾ oz / 20 g) mixed
    fresh herbs such as
    thyme, oregano, basil
    or dill

In a non-corrosive saucepan combine the vinegars, peppercorns and herbs, reserving a few herb sprigs for bottles. Bring to a gentle simmer and cook until flavor has developed, about 15 minutes. Cool. Strain and pour into sterile bottles. Add the reserved herbs and seal. Makes 2 cups (16 fl oz/500 ml).

GARLIC MUSHROOMS

If you haven't used Porcini Vinegar before, you will be delighted by its intense flavor.

- *1 lb (16 oz/500 g) button mushrooms*
- *¼ cup (2 oz/60 g) unsalted butter*
- *2 large garlic cloves, crushed*
- *2 tablespoons Porcini Vinegar (recipe on page 26)*
- *2 tablespoons virgin olive oil*
- *⅓ teaspoon sea salt*
- *⅓ teaspoon freshly ground pepper*
- *2 fresh bay leaves*

Choose mushrooms of the same size. Wipe clean but do not wash. In a deep pan melt the butter, add the mushrooms and garlic and sauté 3–4 minutes. Spoon the entire contents into a bowl. Add the Porcini Vinegar, olive oil, salt and pepper. Crumble in one bay leaf and mix together. Chill in the refrigerator a minimum 2 hours and maximum 2 days. To serve, transfer to a serving platter. Garnish with the remaining bay leaf.

Serves 6

TOMATO AND ORANGE SOUP

Garlic Vinegar adds sharpness to this uncooked soup.

- 2 *ripe oranges, well scrubbed*
- 2 *lb (1 kg) ripe tomatoes, peeled and chopped*
- ½ *small white onion, grated*
- 3½ *cups (28 fl oz / 875 ml) rich chicken stock*
- 2 *tablespoons Garlic Vinegar (recipe on page 26)*
- 1 *tablespoon olive oil*
- 2 *tablespoons chopped fresh chervil*
  Sea salt and cayenne pepper
  Fresh chervil leaves

Using a knife, peel the zest from the oranges and julienne. Remove the membranes and segment the oranges. In a large glass or ceramic bowl combine the orange segments, tomatoes, onion, stock, Garlic Vinegar and olive oil. Mix well and add the chopped chervil, salt and cayenne to taste. Cover and chill 12 hours. To serve, transfer to individual bowls. Garnish with the zest and chervil leaves.

Serves 6

Eggplant Salad with Sun-dried Tomatoes

If fresh mozzarella cheese is not available, you can use any small, round, fresh curd cheese.

10 small rounds mozzarella cheese
2   cups (16 oz / 500 ml) Marinated Eggplant (aubergine)
1   cup (8 oz / 250 g) sun-dried tomatoes, cut into strips
1   garlic clove, slivered
    Basil Vinegar (recipe on page 24)
    Fresh basil leaves

Edge a serving plate with the cheese. Place the Marinated Eggplant and tomato in the center. Top with garlic. To serve, sprinkle with Basil Vinegar to taste. Garnish with the basil leaves.

Marinated Eggplant

1   onion, sliced lengthwise from stem to root
1   carrot, sliced
3   garlic cloves, peeled and crushed
3   tablespoons virgin olive oil
1½ cups (12 fl oz / 375 ml) Basil Vinegar (recipe on page 24)
1½ cups (12 fl oz / 375 ml) water
2   sprigs each fresh thyme, oregano and tarragon
2   fresh bay leaves
4   cardamom pods
1   teaspoon black peppercorns
    Salt and freshly ground pepper
4   globe eggplant (aubergine), sliced
    Extra bay and thyme leaves
    Additional olive oil

In a saucepan sauté the onion, carrot and garlic in the olive oil. Add the Basil Vinegar, water, thyme, oregano, tarragon, bay leaves, cardamom and peppercorns. Salt and pepper to taste. Bring to a boil and simmer several minutes. Place eggplant in a shallow glass dish. Add the marinade, cover and refrigerate overnight. Remove eggplant and place into sterilized preserving jars, tucking extra bay and thyme leaves between layers of the eggplant. Add the additional olive oil to cover. Seal firmly. Store in a cool, dark place 1 month before using. Keeps an additional 6 weeks.

Serves 4–6

MEXICAN RICE SALAD

The traditional flavors of Mexico here enliven a colorful rice salad.

- 3 cups (21 oz/660 g) cooked short grain rice, well chilled
- 2 tomatoes, chopped
- 1 celery stalk, finely diced
- 1 small hot chili, seeded and finely shredded
- ¼ cup (¼ oz/7 g) fresh cilantro leaves
- 1 avocado, halved, pitted and peeled
- 2 tablespoons fresh lime juice
- 2 tablespoons Chili Vinegar (recipe on page 26)
- ¼ cup (2 fl oz/60 ml) olive oil
  Fresh cilantro sprigs

In a serving bowl combine the rice, tomatoes, celery, chili and cilantro. Brush the avocado with 1 tablespoon of the lime juice, slice and reserve half; dice the other half and toss it into the salad. In a separate bowl mix the Chili Vinegar and remaining lime juice and olive oil. Sprinkle over salad and toss. To serve, top salad with the avocado slices and cilantro sprigs.

Serves 6

Garbanzo Bean and Olive Salad

Mild garbanzo beans are balanced here by zesty Orange Vinegar.

2 cups (12 oz / 370 g) cooked or canned garbanzo beans (chick-peas), well drained
1 cup (5 oz / 155 g) imported black olives, pitted and sliced
3 green (spring) onions, finely chopped
1 tablespoon finely chopped fresh cilantro
1 garlic clove, finely chopped
½ teaspoon paprika
⅓ teaspoon chili powder
2 tablespoons virgin olive oil
2 tablespoons Orange Vinegar (recipe on page 25)
Lettuce leaves
Fresh cilantro sprigs

In a large bowl combine the garbanzo beans, olives, onions, chopped cilantro, garlic, paprika, chili powder, olive oil and Orange Vinegar. Toss thoroughly. To serve, transfer to a platter lined with lettuce leaves. Garnish with the cilantro sprigs.

Serves 4–6

CHILLED TROUT WITH WALNUT SAUCE

It is important not to overcook fish. Carefully follow this cooking method to prevent overcooking.

2 *cleaned trout, about ½ lb (8 oz / 250 g) each*
6 *cups (48 fl oz / 1.5 l) water*
¼ *cup (2 fl oz / 60 ml) Tarragon Vinegar (recipe on page 27)*
½ *teaspoon salt*
½ *teaspoon whole peppercorns*
2 *tablespoons chopped shallots*
2 *tablespoons chopped fresh parsley Fresh tarragon leaves*

In a large, shallow saucepan cover the fish with the water, Tarragon Vinegar, salt and peppercorns. Bring to a boil, remove from the heat and cover the pan tightly with foil. Leave the fish to cook 8–10 minutes, quickly turning after 5 minutes and replacing the foil. Drain fish and reserve the cooking liquid for the Walnut Sauce. Chill fish in the refrigerator until serving. To serve, place fish onto a serving platter. Sprinkle with the shallots and parsley. Top with the Walnut Sauce. Garnish with the tarragon leaves.

WALNUT SAUCE

1 *cup (4 oz / 120 g) finely ground shelled walnuts*
3 *garlic cloves, peeled and crushed*
⅓ *teaspoon salt*
2 *tablespoons chopped fresh chives*
3 *tablespoons Tarragon Vinegar (recipe on page 27)*
1 *tablespoon chopped fresh tarragon leaves Cayenne pepper*

In a medium bowl mix the walnuts, garlic, salt, chives, Tarragon Vinegar, tarragon leaves and cayenne to taste. Whisk in enough of the reserved poaching liquid to create a smooth and creamy sauce. If a richer sauce is desired, add 2 tablespoons of heavy (double) cream. Cover and chill until serving time.

Serves 2

Smoked Salmon and Asparagus Salad

The happy marriage of lemon juice and fish is a familiar one, but here, a touch of orange juice provides a lively variation. If a more intense walnut flavor is desired, substitute 1 cup of walnut oil for the mixture of walnut and olive oil.

1 *lb (16 oz / 500 g) small asparagus spears, trimmed*

4 *green (spring) onions, blanched*

2 *cups (2 oz / 60 g) mixed baby salad greens*

¾ *lb (12 oz / 375 g) smoked salmon, thinly sliced*

2 *oranges, peeled, membranes removed and segmented*

Cook the asparagus spears in lightly salted boiling water, about 8 minutes. Drain and refresh with cold water. Divide the asparagus into 4 bundles and tie each bundle with an onion. To serve, place the greens on a serving platter. Place the salmon and asparagus bundles on the greens. Garnish with the orange segments. Use the Walnut Orange Mayonnaise for dipping.

Walnut Orange Mayonnaise

2 *egg yolks*

½ *teaspoon Dijon mustard*

¼ *teaspoon salt*

⅛ *teaspoon pepper*

3 *tablespoons Orange Vinegar (recipe on page 25)*

½ *cup (4 fl oz / 125 ml) each virgin olive oil and walnut oil, combined*

1 *tablespoon orange juice*

In a small bowl blend the egg yolks, mustard, salt and pepper. Using an electric mixer beat vigorously until light and fluffy. While continuing to beat, alternately add 2 teaspoons of the Orange Vinegar and ¼ cup of the combined oils, one drop at a time. Continuing to beat, add the remaining Orange Vinegar, orange juice and oils, pouring each in a thin trickle. Beat until the oil is incorporated and the mayonnaise has thickened. If the mayonnaise is too thick, beat in a tablespoon of boiling water. Chill until serving time.

Serves 4

FINES HERBES CHICKEN SALAD

Traditional *fines herbes* is a combination of tarragon, parsley, chervil and chives often used in French cooking.

- 1 cup (1 oz/30 g) red oakleaf lettuce
- 1 cup (1 oz/30 g) arugula leaves
- 1 cup (1 oz/30 g) baby spinach leaves
- 1 cup (1 oz/30 g) curly endive leaves
- 6 anchovy fillets, very finely chopped
- 2 cups (12 oz/370 g) roast chicken breast, diced
- ½ red bell pepper (capsicum), finely julienned
  Fresh tarragon sprigs

Prepare the salad greens by washing, drying well and crisping in a sealed container in the refrigerator. In a large bowl, combine the salad greens, anchovies and chicken. Spoon on sufficient Fines Herbes Mayonnaise to moisten the ingredients and toss lightly. To serve, garnish with the red pepper and tarragon sprigs.

FINES HERBES MAYONNAISE

- 1¼ cups (10 fl oz/310 ml) mayonnaise
- 2 tablespoons finely chopped fresh tarragon
- 2 tablespoons finely chopped fresh parsley
- 2 tablespoons finely chopped fresh chervil
- 2 tablespoons finely chopped fresh chives
- 2 tablespoons Tarragon Vinegar (recipe on page 27)
- 1 garlic clove, peeled and finely chopped

In a medium bowl whisk together the mayonnaise, tarragon, parsley, chervil, chives, Tarragon Vinegar and garlic. Chill until serving time.

Serves 4

DUCK BREASTS WITH SPICED CHERRIES

Serve this rich poultry dish with a robust wild rice, vegetable medley.

- 4 6 oz (185 g) small duck breasts, boned
- ½ teaspoon salt
- ½ teaspoon freshly ground pepper
- ⅓ cup (3 oz / 90 g) unsalted butter
- 1 shallot, finely chopped
- 16 small mushrooms, stems removed
- 2 tablespoons Orange Vinegar (recipe on page 25)
- 3 tablespoons rich chicken stock

Sprinkle the duck breasts with salt and pepper. In a heavy frying pan heat the butter and brown the breasts on both sides, then sauté until breasts are tender but still pink inside, about 5 minutes per side. Remove the breasts from the pan and keep warm. In the same pan, in the retained butter, sauté the shallot and mushrooms. Add the Spiced Cherries and deglaze the pan with the Orange Vinegar. Add the stock and cook over high heat 2 minutes. To serve, slice the breasts diagonally and place on a serving platter. Top with the sauce and Spiced Cherries.

SPICED CHERRIES

- 20 ripe cherries, pitted
- ½ cup (4 fl oz / 125 ml) red wine vinegar
- 1 tablespoon brown sugar
- 2 tablespoons water
- 3 whole cloves
- 1 whole star anise
- 4 whole peppercorns

In a saucepan combine the cherries, red wine vinegar, brown sugar, water, cloves, star anise and peppercorns. Simmer very gently until cherries are tender, about 5 minutes. Drain and discard liquid. Put the cherries into a sterilized container and seal. Refrigerate up to 1 week before using.

Serves 4–6

MARINATED GRILLED LAMB

This marinade is equally delicious for vegetables such as bell peppers, corn, tomatoes and zucchini. Roast them over hot coals for 10 minutes.

- *1   3 lb (1.5 kg) leg of lamb, boned*
- *½ cup (4 fl oz / 125 ml) virgin olive oil*
- *2   tablespoons Mixed Herb Vinegar (recipe on page 27)*
- *¼ cup (⅜ oz / 10 g) chopped mixed herbs*
- *⅓ teaspoon chili powder*
- *1   tablespoon Worcestershire sauce*

Put the lamb into a dish, flattening it so that the meat thickness is as even as possible. In a bowl combine the olive oil, Mixed Herb Vinegar, herbs, chili powder and Worcestershire sauce. Pour the marinade over the meat. Cover and refrigerate 12 hours, turning the meat occasionally. Prepare a fire in a barbecue grill. Cook the lamb over heated coals, allowing 10 minutes per pound. Baste often with the marinade.

Serves 6

RASPBERRY CHICKEN

Raspberry Vinegar makes a lively
sauce for traditional fried chicken.

- 2 *cups (16 fl oz / 500 ml) olive oil*
- 1 *cup (5 oz / 155 g) all-purpose (plain) flour*
- ½ *teaspoon salt*
- ⅓ *teaspoon white pepper*
- 4 *half chicken breasts*
- 1 *tablespoon Raspberry Vinegar (recipe on page 25)*
- ⅓ *cup (3 fl oz / 80 ml) rich chicken stock*
- ½ *cup (2 oz / 64 g) ripe raspberries*
- ½ *teaspoon sugar*

In a heavy frying pan heat the olive oil
until hot. In a medium bowl sift together the flour, salt and pepper. Dredge
the chicken, place into the oil, cover
and cook 10 minutes. Turn pieces and
cook, uncovered, 15 minutes. Remove
the chicken. Drain the oil. Deglaze the
pan with the Raspberry Vinegar. Add
the stock, raspberries and sugar.
Simmer about 3 minutes. To serve,
place chicken on individual plates and
top with the sauce.

Serves 4

CHERRY FRUIT CAKE

Take this lovely cake on a picnic or give it as a holiday gift.

1⅔ cups (8½ oz / 275 g) whole-wheat (wholemeal) flour

1⅔ cups (8½ oz / 275 g) all-purpose (plain) flour

1½ teaspoons nutmeg
     Zest of 1 orange, grated
     Zest of 1 lemon, grated

1 cup (7 oz / 220 g) soft brown sugar

½ lb (8 oz / 250 g) glacé cherries

¾ lb (12 oz / 375 g) mixed dried fruits

⅓ cup (1½ oz / 45 g) ground almonds

¾ cup (6 fl oz / 180 ml) sunflower oil

1¼ cups (10 fl oz / 310 ml) milk

1 teaspoon baking soda (bicarbonate of soda)

3 tablespoons Strawberry Vinegar (recipe on page 25)

¼ cup (1 oz / 30 g) sliced almonds

Preheat an oven to 300°F (150°C). Grease and line an 8-inch (20-cm) round by 2-inch (5-cm) deep cake pan. In a mixing bowl sift together the flours and nutmeg. Mix in the orange and lemon zests, sugar, cherries, dried fruits and ground almonds. Add the sunflower oil and milk and stir well. In a small bowl dissolve the baking soda into the Strawberry Vinegar and stir thoroughly. Quickly stir into the flour mixture. Spoon into the pan and sprinkle the sliced almonds on top. Bake until a toothpick inserted into the cake comes out clean, 1¾–2 hours. Turn out of the pan and cool on a wire rack.

Makes one 8-inch cake

All kinds of pickles, dressings and savory jellies owe their memorable flavor to the fruity bouquet and sharp tang of apple cider vinegar. Still more recipes benefit from a splash of this vinegar—particularly those featuring pork and red meats, which show a natural affinity for apples.

Carefully read labels in search of cider vinegar that had its start as real aged cider made from whole apples; some inexpensive commercial products are made from peels and cores.

Unlike wine vinegar infused with fruit, fruit vinegars are made from the aged wine of the fruit itself. Apricot, pear, plum and gooseberry are popular fruit vinegars.

Both cider and fruit vinegars take on a hint of the color of their fruit. They should be free of sediment.

COLD SPICED BEEF

Make sandwiches with this meat topped with spicy Green Tomato Relish (recipe on page 55).

5 *lb (2.5 kg) corned (brined) beef, trimmed of excess fat*
1 *carrot, coarsely chopped*
2 *celery stalks, sliced*
1 *large onion, sliced*
1 *teaspoon whole peppercorns*
3 *whole cloves*
1 *cinnamon stick*
1 *orange, halved*
 Bouquet garni
⅓ *cup (3 fl oz/80 ml) cider vinegar*

Put the beef into a large pot. Add the carrot, celery, onion, peppercorns, cloves, cinnamon, orange and bouquet garni. Pour in the cider vinegar and water to cover. Bring to a boil, reduce heat and simmer 1½–2 hours, occasionally skimming surface during cooking. Cool. Remove the meat, cover with foil, top with something heavy and leave overnight. (Pressing ensures that the meat slices easily.) To serve, thinly slice the meat.

Serves 8

Tajine of Lamb

Serve this exotic stew from Morocco
on a bed of couscous.

¼ cup (2 fl oz/60 ml) olive oil
2 lb (1 kg) lamb shoulder, cut into
1-inch (2.5-cm) cubes
1 onion, finely chopped
3 garlic cloves, peeled and crushed
1 teaspoon ground ginger
2 teaspoons chopped fresh tarragon
1 teaspoon ground cinnamon
2 cups (16 fl oz/500 ml) water
1 cup (6 oz/185 g) chopped
dried pears
3 tablespoons honey
2 tablespoons pear vinegar
2 tablespoons each raisins and
blanched almonds

In a saucepan heat the olive oil. Brown
the lamb, about 5 minutes per side.
Add the onion, garlic, ginger, tarragon,
cinnamon and water. Cover, bring to a
boil, reduce heat and simmer until
lamb is tender, 1½ hours. Stir in the
pears, honey and pear vinegar. Simmer
15 minutes, stirring often. To serve,
sprinkle with the raisins and almonds.

Serves 6–8

RED CABBAGE AND APPLE CASSEROLE

Serve this sharp-tasting side dish with rich meats such as the Savory Steak Casserole (recipe on page 56).

1   small red cabbage, thinly sliced
2   tablespoons butter
1   eating apple, peeled, cored and
      thinly sliced
1   small onion, finely chopped
⅓   teaspoon grated nutmeg
      Salt and cayenne pepper
3   teaspoons dark brown sugar
⅓   teaspoon ground cloves
⅓   teaspoon ground cinnamon
2   tablespoons cider vinegar

Soak the cabbage in cold water, about 15 minutes. Lightly drain the cabbage and place into a large saucepan. Add the butter, apple, onion and nutmeg. Add salt and cayenne to taste. Cover and cook over low heat 45 minutes, stirring occasionally to prevent the cabbage from sticking. Stir in the sugar, cloves, cinnamon and cider vinegar and cook an additional 5 minutes.

Serves 6–8

SPICED FRUIT COMPOTE

For a richer dessert, top the fruit with whipped cream and grated nutmeg.

- 8 *dried prunes, pitted*
- 8 *dried apricots, halved*
- ½ *cup (3 oz / 92 g) raisins*
- 2 *dried peaches, quartered*
- ½ each *orange and lemon, unpeeled*
- 1½ *cups (12 fl oz / 375 ml) white wine*
- ½ *cup (6 oz / 185 g) honey*
- 1 *cinnamon stick*
- 4 *cloves*
- 1 *star anise*
- 1½ *tablespoons apricot vinegar*
- 2 *pears, peeled, quartered and cored*
- ½ *tablespoon* each *julienned lemon and orange zest*

In a saucepan combine the prunes, apricots, raisins, peaches, orange and lemon. Add the wine, honey, cinnamon, cloves and star anise. Simmer 20 minutes. Remove from heat, discard the anise and chill overnight. Remove the orange, lemon, clove and cinnamon. Add the apricot vinegar, pears and zest. Chill several hours before serving.

Serves 4–6

MALT VINEGAR

In England until the mid-17th century, vinegar made from beer was known, appropriately, as "alegar." The name has changed, but the product remains a staple in that country, adding its robust taste and tang as a condiment for fish and chips and as an ingredient in fruit chutneys, relishes and other generously spiced dishes.

Because the vinegar flavor will dissipate when exposed to air, sprinkle it on foods just before eating. Today's malt vinegar, as its name might suggest, is not strictly speaking made from beer or ale. Malt vinegar starts as gyle, a crude brew of malted barley. Acetobacters are introduced and the brew is filtered and slowly matured to produce a clear vinegar. That vinegar is colored with caramel to a deep brown color reminiscent of a hand-pulled pint in a pub.

GREEN TOMATO RELISH

Ripe tomatoes may be used if green ones are not available.

6 lb (3 kg) green tomatoes, chopped
1 lb (16 oz / 500 g) white onions, chopped
1 tablespoon salt
2 red or green bell peppers (capsicums), stemmed, seeded and finely chopped
4¾ cups (38 fl oz / 1.18 l) malt vinegar
3 cups (1½ lb / 750 g) sugar
1 tablespoon curry powder
1 teaspoon powdered cumin
½ teaspoon coarsely ground pepper
2 tablespoons cornstarch
3 tablespoons mustard powder

In a large ceramic or glass bowl combine the tomatoes and onions. Sprinkle with the salt, cover and leave overnight in a cool place, but do not refrigerate. Drain and discard the liquid. In a large saucepan mix the tomatoes, onions, peppers, 4 cups of the malt vinegar, sugar, curry powder, cumin and pepper. Bring to a boil, reduce heat to a simmer and cook, stirring often, 2–2½ hours. In a separate bowl blend together the cornstarch, mustard powder and remaining malt vinegar. Stir until smooth. Add to the saucepan. Bring to a boil and continue to cook, stirring constantly, until the relish thickens, about 20 minutes. Reduce heat and simmer, stirring often, for an additional 20 minutes. Ladle into sterilized jars and seal while hot. Store unopened in a cool, dark place up to 12 months. Refrigerate after opening.

Makes about 8 medium-sized jars

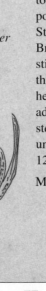

SAVORY STEAK CASSEROLE

Inexpensive, flavorful flank steak makes this old-fashioned dish an excellent value.

- 2 tablespoons all-purpose (plain) flour
- ½ teaspoon salt
- ½ teaspoon ground mace
- ⅓ teaspoon freshly ground pepper
  Cayenne pepper
- 1½ lb (750 g) flank steak
- 1 large onion, thinly sliced
- 1 tablespoon Worcestershire sauce
- 1 tablespoon malt vinegar
- 1 tablespoon brown sugar
- 3 tablespoons chopped fresh parsley
- ½ cup (4 fl oz / 125 ml) beef stock

Preheat an oven to 250°F (120°C). In a bowl combine the flour, salt, mace, pepper and cayenne to taste. Rub the mixture all over the steak. Put the meat into a baking dish. Surround with the onion slices. In a bowl combine the Worcestershire sauce, malt vinegar, sugar, 2 tablespoons of the parsley and stock. Pour the mixture over the meat and onion and cover tightly with foil. Bake 3 hours. Check often to ensure liquid has not evaporated and, if necessary, add water. To serve, cut the meat into portions and place onto individual plates. Garnish with the remaining parsley.

Serves 6

RICE VINEGAR

Vinegar's origins in Asia may be traced back more than three thousand years, when records show the Chinese produced it from rice wine. Today's cooks can choose from four different types of rice vinegar. That designated "red" rice vinegar is a clean-tasting product most often used as a dip for fried foods. Mildly acidic "black" rice vinegar, sweetened with sugar and subtly spiced, is also used for dipping and has a color and complexity reminiscent of balsamic vinegar.

"White" rice vinegar, pale gold in color, usually provides the sour element in sweet-and-sour dishes. The slightly sweet and subtly acidic unseasoned Japanese product known as *su* is a key ingredient in sushi rice.

Experiment with various types as you discover cooking with rice vinegar.

PICKLED SHRIMP

Shrimp is a splendid appetizer or light first course.

1 cup (8 fl oz / 250 ml) rice vinegar
1 small onion, thinly sliced
¾ teaspoon red chili flakes
2 teaspoons sugar
¼ teaspoon cracked peppercorns
4 whole cloves
24 raw shrimp (prawns), peeled and deveined
¼ cup (3 oz / 10 g) chopped fresh dill
24 thick slices cucumber
    Fresh dill sprigs

In a saucepan combine the rice vinegar, onion, chili flakes, sugar, peppercorns and cloves. Bring to a boil, cover, reduce heat and simmer 10 minutes. Add the shrimp and return to a boil. Cook until the shrimp turn pink, about 5 minutes. Remove from heat and transfer to a bowl to cool. Stir in the chopped dill and chill overnight. To serve, drain the shrimp, arranging each one on a slice of cucumber. Garnish each shrimp with a dill sprig.

Serves 4

ASIAN CUCUMBER SALAD

Mild rice vinegar makes the perfect medium for an Asian salad dressing.

- *2 cucumbers, peeled and thinly sliced*
- *2 tablespoons rice vinegar*
- *1 tablespoon dark brown sugar*
- *1 tablespoon light soy sauce*
- *1 tablespoon sesame oil*
- *½ teaspoon salt*
- *1 fresh red chili, about 1-inch (2.5-cm) long, seeded and chopped*
- *Fresh chervil sprigs*

In a bowl combine the cucumbers, rice vinegar, sugar, soy sauce, oil and salt. Sprinkle with the chili. Toss well. Chill in the refrigerator at least 2 hours before serving. To serve, arrange on individual plates. Garnish with the chervil sprigs.

Serves 2

BUCKWHEAT NOODLES WITH SNOW PEAS

Used in Chinese cooking, traditional five-spice powder is a combination of star anise, anise seed, clove, cinnamon and Sichuan peppercorns. It is available in Asian food shops.

½ cup (4 fl oz / 125 ml) light soy sauce
¼ cup (2 fl oz / 60 ml) rich chicken stock
2 teaspoons sugar
3 tablespoons sesame seeds, toasted
1 lb (500 g) dried buckwheat noodles
⅓ lb (6 oz / 185 g) snow peas, trimmed and cut into diagonal strips
4 green (spring) onions, cut diagonally into ½-inch (12-mm) pieces
2 tablespoons sesame oil
1 tablespoon rice vinegar
⅓ teaspoon five-spice powder
Fresh cilantro sprigs

In the work bowl of a food processor or blender combine the soy sauce, stock, sugar and half of the sesame seeds. Blend until smooth. Cook the noodles in boiling water according to package directions until al dente and drain. In a serving bowl combine the noodles and soy sauce mixture. Cool, stirring occasionally. Blanch the snow peas in boiling water 2–3 minutes, drain and refresh in cold water. Add the peas and onions to the noodles. In a small bowl whisk together the sesame oil, rice vinegar and five-spice powder. To serve, pour dressing over room temperature noodles and toss. Garnish with the cilantro and remaining sesame seeds.

Serves 4

I N D E X

Apples, 50
Apricot vinegar, 51
Asparagus, 37

Balsamic vinegar, 9, 12-13
Basil vinegar, 24, 30
Beans, garbanzo, 33
Beef
  corned, 48
  flank steak, 56
Beets, 13
Bell peppers, 10
Bruschetta, 10

Cabbage, red, 50
Cake, cherry, 44
Casseroles, 50, 56
Champagne vinegar, 9, 15-16
Cherries, spiced, 41
Chicken
  poached, 16
  raspberry, 43
  smoked, 22
Chili vinegar, 26, 32
Cider vinegar, 46, 48, 50
Cucumbers, 61

Desserts, 44, 51
Duck
  roast, 19
  sautéed, 41

Eggplant, marinated, 30

Entrees, 15-16, 19, 21-23,
  28, 34, 37, 41-43, 48,
  50, 56, 60, 62

Figs, dried, 23
Fruit vinegar, 46

Garlic vinegar, 26, 29
Grapes, pickled, 22

Lamb
  grilled, 42
  tajine of, 49
Lemon vinegar, 24, 33

Malt vinegar, 52, 55-56
Mayonnaise
  Champagne, 16
  fines herbes, 38
  walnut orange, 37
Mixed herb vinegar, 27, 42
Mushrooms, garlic, 28

Noodles, 62

Olives, 33
Orange vinegar, 25, 37, 41
Oranges, 29
Oysters, 15

Pear vinegar, 49
Porcini vinegar, 26, 28
Pork, 23

Raspberry vinegar, 25, 43
Red wine vinegar, 9, 19, 23,
  27, 41
Relish, green tomato, 55
Rice vinegar, 58, 60-62

Salads
  Asian cucumber, 61
  asparagus, 37
  chicken, 38
  eggplant, 30
  garbanzo beans, 33
  Italian bread, 12
  Mexican rice, 32
  salmon, smoked, 37
Sauces
  champagne vinegar, 15
  walnut, 34
Sausages, Italian, 21
Sherry vinegar, 9, 14
Shrimp, 60
Snow peas, 62
Soups
  beet, 13
  tomato and orange, 29
Stews, 49
Strawberry vinegar, 25, 44

Tarragon vinegar, 27, 34, 38
Tomatoes, 12, 29, 30
Trout, 34

White wine vinegar, 9, 21-22,
  24-27